The Golden Girls of Rio

To my gold medal coaches... My Parents...
Vernon & Jacquetta Smith

Sky Pony Press books may be purchased in bulk at special discounts for sales promotion, corporate gifts, fund-raising, or educational purposes. Special editions can also be created to specifications. For details, contact the Special Sales Department, Sky Pony Press, 307 West 36th Street, 11th Floor, New York, NY 10018 or info@skyhorsepublishing.com.

Sky Pony® is a registered trademark of Skyhorse Publishing, Inc.®, a Delaware corporation.

Visit our website at www.skyponypress.com.

10 9 8 7 6 5 4 3 2 1

Library of Congress Cataloging-in-Publication Data is available on file.

Cover design and illustration by Nikkolas Smith

Print ISBN: 978-1-5107-2247-7
Ebook ISBN: 978-1-5107-2248-4

Printed in the United States of America

The Golden Girls of Rio

NIKKOLAS SMITH

Sky Pony Press
New York

We Are Girls.

We Are Golden.

We Are America!

But their golden path to the Olympics
began many years ago, when they were...

very YOUNG! ...and full of dreams.
So how did it all begin?

Kathleen
Baker

Lilly
King

Dana
Vollmer

Simone
Manuel

Katie
Ledecky

Michelle
Carter

Aly

Dana

Lilly

Laurie

Katie

Gabby

Michelle

Kathleen

Madison

Simone B.

Simone M.

Across America, many young girls were discovering new sports and LOVING it. Let's follow the paths of the girls who won Olympic GOLD.

Simone Biles   Aly Raisman   Laurie Hernandez   Gabby Douglas   Madison Kocian

The girls were different in many ways, but they ALL had one thing in common…they wanted to be the best.

They understood that they must train, work hard, and never give up, in order to win!

Our story begins with two future champions, born three days apart.

Little Simone Biles, from Spring, TX.

And young Katie Ledecky, who grew up in Washington, DC.

They were both so very full of energy and life!

Out west in San Jose, CA,
little Michelle Carter was always looking up to her father.
As a professional athlete and Olympic medalist himself,
she followed in his footsteps,
day by day.

Once while on a class field trip, six-year-old Simone was introduced to the world of gymnastics. It showed her that she could be small but still quite powerful.

Her goal from that moment forward was to jump, flip, and fly higher than any boy or girl.

Young Katie Ledecky was born into a family of swimmers.
Would she be as great as her big brother?
She decided to swim, anyway.
Not to prove anything.
But simply because she loved to swim.

Another Golden Girl was following in the steps of her older brothers, who were also swimmers. Simone Manuel started going to the pool with them in their hometown of Sugar Land, Texas. Quickly a coach saw her talent and began training her. She was only three years old!

Simone Biles was now eleven years old and tumbling all over Texas, with the goal to one day compete for an Olympic gold medal. She met friends along the way who shared the same dream.

One of these friends was
Laurie Hernandez, a young gymnast
from New Jersey!

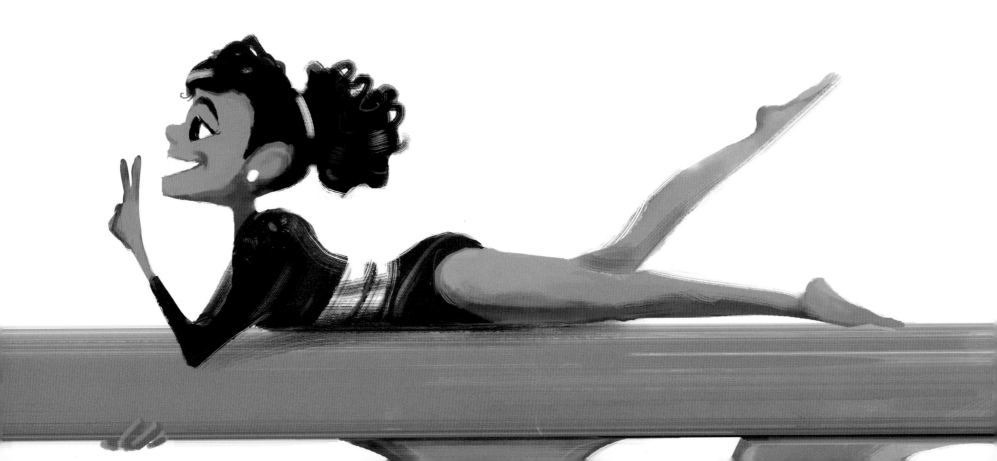

Like all the other girls, Laurie worked very hard
to be perfect on all of her events.

Katie had grown much taller
(and faster!) than most kids her age…
She started to meet many talented swimmers
who were also very fast.

"Hi, I'm Simone Manuel!"

These girls knew it would be tough to rise to the top, but they remained focused. No matter what obstacles threw them off track, they worked hard to reach their goal. They worked hard to reach their gold.

The girls were competing
all across the nation and
winning shiny awards.
Now that they were the best
in the country, it was
time for the world
stage…

…the
Olympics.

The girls proudly
reached their destination.
They were thrilled to see so many other
USA athletes who also shared
their golden dream.

The competition was strong.
Butterflies were floating in their stomachs,
as they realized that all of their training
and competition led to this
exciting moment.

Michelle took a deep breath, and launched her shot into the sky… Golden!

The swim team raced…
Gold, gold, gold!

The gymnastics team performed…
Gold, gold, gold!

The five girls received more gold
medals than any other gymnastics
team in the history of America.

They are the
Golden Girls!

Michelle Carter
First American woman to win
gold in shot put.

Katie Ledecky
Word record holder in the
women's 400-, 800-, and
1,500-meter freestyle.

They made
America proud.

Simone Biles
Most decorated American
gymnast of all time.

Simone Manuel
First African American woman
to medal in an individual
swimming event.

"You're never too young or old to reach your gold."